SPORTS GOATs:
THE GREATEST OF ALL TIME

GOATs OF BASEBALL

BY ANTHONY K. HEWSON

SportsZone

An Imprint of Abdo Publishing
abdobooks.com

T0019620

abdobooks.com

Published by Abdo Publishing, a division of ABDO, PO Box 398166, Minneapolis, Minnesota 55439. Copyright © 2022 by Abdo Consulting Group, Inc. International copyrights reserved in all countries. No part of this book may be reproduced in any form without written permission from the publisher. SportsZone™ is a trademark and logo of Abdo Publishing.

Printed in the United States of America, North Mankato, Minnesota.
102021
012022

THIS BOOK CONTAINS
RECYCLED MATERIALS

Cover Photo: Mike Carlson/AP Images
Interior Photos: George Grantham Bain Collection/Library of Congress, 4, 4–5; Bettmann/Getty Images, 6, 7; Kathy Willens/AP Images, 7; Charles M. Conlon/Sporting News/Getty Images, 8, 9; AP Images, 10, 10–11, 16, 17, 20, 20–21, 22, 23, 28–29, 29, 32, 32–33; The Rucker Archive/Icon Sportswire, 12, 13; Mark Rucker/Transcendental Graphics/Getty Images Sport/Getty Images, 14, 14–15; STF/AP Images, 18, 19; Science History Images/Alamy, 24, 25; Harold Filan/AP Images , 26, 26–27; Bob Daugherty/AP Images, 30–31, 31; Ben Margot/AP Images , 34, 35; Eric Risberg/AP Images, 36, 36–37; John Cordes/Icon Sportswire/AP Images, 38, 38–39; Jeff Roberson/AP Images, 40, 41; Elaine Thompson/AP Images, 42, 42–43

Editor: Charlie Beattie
Series Designer: Jake Nordby

Library of Congress Control Number: 2021941617

Publisher's Cataloging-in-Publication Data

Names: Hewson, Anthony K., author.
Title: GOATs of baseball / by Anthony K. Hewson
Description: Minneapolis, Minnesota : Abdo Publishing, 2022 | Series: Sports GOATs: The greatest of all time | Includes online resources and index.
Identifiers: ISBN 9781532196485 (lib. bdg.) | ISBN 9781644947081 (pbk.) | ISBN 9781098218294 (ebook)
Subjects: LCSH: Baseball--Juvenile literature. | Baseball players--Juvenile literature. | Baseball players--Rating of--United States--Juvenile literature. | Baseball--Records--United States--Juvenile literature. | Professional athletes--Juvenile literature.
Classification: DDC 796.357--dc23

TABLE OF
CONTENTS

CY YOUNG

Baseball looked quite different back when Denton True "Cy" Young first took the mound. Young debuted for the Cleveland Spiders in 1890. In those days, teams used fewer pitchers. And the pitcher that started the game often finished it.

In his first full season in 1891, Young started 46 games. He completed 43 of them. Those numbers are unheard of in Major League Baseball (MLB) today. These days a star pitcher might complete three games in a season. Most pitchers don't complete any at all.

In an era when aces didn't need a variety of pitches, Young was known for a dominant fastball. Hall of Fame shortstop Honus Wagner called it the greatest fastball he'd ever seen. As Young got older and couldn't throw as hard, he developed two different curveballs. He also became a master of control.

In Young's time, the mound was moved farther back, to its current distance from home plate, 60 feet, 6 inches (18.4 m). Hitters also could now foul off as many pitches as they wanted without striking out. Both changes made it easier for hitters. But Young remained dominant.

In addition to pitching a lot, Young also won a lot. His 511 career wins are the most in baseball history. The second-place pitcher has 417. No one is likely to ever come close to Young's record.

Young died in 1955. Around the same time, MLB was looking for a way to honor the best pitcher each season. In 1956 it announced the first annual Cy Young Award winner. The award is given annually to the best pitcher in the American League (AL) and National League (NL).

FAST FACT

In the earliest days of
baseball, some pitchers
threw even more often
than Young. In 1884
Old Hoss Radbourn
started 73 games for the
Providence Grays. He
completed them all.
He won 60 of them.

Cy Young started 815 games in his career and completed 749 of them.

Honus Wagner won his first batting title at age 26. He won his last when he was 37 years old.

HONUS WAGNER

In the early 1900s, Honus Wagner's hitting ability scared opposing players. One of the most dominant pitchers of the time was Christy Mathewson, who always looked for a weakness in hitters. As a young pitcher, Mathewson once asked his catcher the best way to attack Wagner. The catcher said the best way was to walk him.

Standing at the plate, Wagner didn't look like one of the most fearsome hitters in baseball. He used an unusual grip, with his hands far apart on the bat. But it worked for Wagner. He had a .300 or better batting average every year from 1899 to 1913. He led the NL in batting average eight times. No one else would win eight NL batting titles until Tony Gwynn reached that number in 1997. Wagner was also an outstanding shortstop and baserunner. He stole 723 career bases.

Fans loved Wagner's exciting playing style. He became one of baseball's first true superstars. Wagner was the first player to have his own signature on a baseball bat. He also appeared on some of the first baseball cards. One of Wagner's cards was the rarest and most valuable in history. It sold in 2020 for $3.25 million.

Wagner retired in 1917. He had 3,420 career hits and a lifetime .328 batting average. In 1936 he was inducted into the first class of the Baseball Hall of Fame.

Wagner's rare "T206" baseball card has sold for millions of dollars throughout the years.

WAGNER, PITTSBURG

Ty Cobb shows off his aggressive style of base running as he slides into third in a 1909 game against the New York Yankees.

TY COBB

During Ty Cobb's career in the early 1900s, he was known as "the Georgia Peach." But there was nothing peachy about his approach to the game of baseball. Cobb was known as an aggressive and fiercely competitive player. The numbers he put up in baseball's early years remain among the best of all time.

Cobb grew up in Royston, Georgia. His childhood was filled with baseball but also tragedy. His mother killed his father when Cobb was 18 and in his first year with the Detroit Tigers. Cobb vowed to always play his hardest so that he wouldn't let his father down.

Cobb could hit for power. But he also used his speed to get on base any way he could. He was a gifted hitter. From 1907 to 1919, he won the AL batting title in 12 of 13 seasons. After hitting .238 his rookie year, Cobb never hit under .300 again. He hit over .400 three times. His combination of hitting, speed, and power made him one of the greatest players of his day.

After hitting .323 at the age of 41 in 1928, Cobb retired. He did so with 4,189 career hits. That was far and away the most of all time. His record would not even be challenged for nearly 60 years. In 1936 he became an inaugural member of the Hall of Fame.

FAST FACT

Cobb was originally credited with 4,191 career hits. Pete Rose broke Cobb's record with his 4,192nd hit on September 11, 1985. But later research showed two of Cobb's hits were counted twice. MLB officially still credits Cobb with 4,191.

WALTER JOHNSON

Walter Johnson was working for a telephone company in Idaho when the Washington Senators came calling in 1907. Pitching in the Idaho State League, Johnson hadn't allowed a run in 75 innings. He was so good, the Senators manager joked that all the team would need was Johnson and a catcher.

Johnson wasn't quite that dominant. But he was close. He struck out 3,509 batters in his career. No one else reached 3,000 until Bob Gibson did it in 1974.

Johnson piled up all sorts of staggering numbers. He won 417 games. He won 20 games in a season 12 times. No other player has recorded both 400 wins and 3,500 strikeouts. And perhaps most impressive of all, 531 of his 666 career starts were complete games.

Johnson was an intimidating presence on the mound. He was one of baseball's first power pitchers. His pitches felt like a speeding freight train to hitters, earning him the nickname "Big Train." But Johnson was far from intimidating as a person. He was known for his good sportsmanship. Johnson never argued with umpires or threw at hitters. He was never in trouble off the field and was a good teammate.

After retiring, Johnson got into politics, and he became a broadcaster. He lived on a farm near Washington, DC. In 1936 Johnson was elected to the first class of the Hall of Fame.

Walter Johnson's blazing fastball helped him record 110 shutouts in his MLB career.

Baseball's first true power hitter, Babe Ruth broke the MLB single-season home run mark four times in his career.

BABE RUTH

Home runs were not a big part of baseball when Babe Ruth first reached the majors in 1914. That year the AL leader hit just nine. Four years later, as a young Boston Red Sox pitcher and outfielder, Ruth slugged 11 balls out of the park. That was good enough to tie for the MLB lead.

Ruth soon ushered in a new era. In 1919 Ruth set a record with 29 homers. Ruth would break his own record three more times.

After his breakthrough year in 1919, Ruth was sold to the New York Yankees. Now playing outfield full time, his home run pace only increased. In his first season as a Yankee, Ruth belted 54 home runs. That was more than most entire teams hit that season.

Fans had never seen a hitter like Ruth. He was baseball's first true slugger. He knew that fans came out just to see him hit home runs.

Ruth broke his record again in 1921 with 59 homers. But his greatest season came in 1927. As part of the Yankees' famed "Murderers' Row" lineup, Ruth slugged 60 home runs. That record stood for 34 years.

In 22 seasons, Ruth hit 714 career home runs. No one would challenge that record until the 1970s. Even 100 years later, Ruth remains an iconic slugger of baseball history.

FAST FACT

Another Yankee was the first to break Ruth's single-season home run record. Roger Maris finished with 61 homers in 1961.

LOU GEHRIG

In the eighth inning of a game on June 1, 1925, New York Yankees manager Miller Huggins needed a pinch hitter. He asked backup first baseman Lou Gehrig to bat for Pee-Wee Wanninger. Appearing in just his twelfth game of the season, Gehrig flew out to left off Washington Senators pitcher Walter Johnson.

The next day, starting first baseman Wally Pipp had a headache. Pipp also hadn't been playing well. Huggins put Gehrig in the lineup to try to change the team's fortunes. Gehrig didn't come out of the lineup for the next 14 years.

Gehrig played a record 2,130 games in a row. He earned the nickname "the Iron Horse" for his durability. But Gehrig was more than just durable. He was a great all-around hitter who had nearly 500 career home runs. He is one of just 10 players to lead his league in home runs, runs batted in (RBI), and batting average in the same season. That achievement is known as "the Triple Crown."

Gehrig started the 1939 season hitting just .143. On May 2, he took himself out of the lineup. He hadn't been feeling well, and it was affecting his performance.

Gehrig would never play again. He was diagnosed with amyotrophic lateral sclerosis (ALS). The muscular disease would become better known as Lou Gehrig's disease. The diagnosis forced Gehrig to retire immediately. He was elected to the Hall of Fame in 1939. Gehrig died two years later.

After playing 2,130 consecutive games, Lou Gehrig held the title of baseball's "Iron Man" for nearly 60 years.

FAST FACT

In December 2020, MLB chose to include Negro League records as official MLB statistics. That put Gibson's career .365 average among the top 10 in baseball history.

Despite being one of the greatest hitters of any era, Josh Gibson never got the chance to play in MLB.

JOSH GIBSON

Certain fans who saw Josh Gibson play were reminded of another great player at the time. Many would refer to him as "the Black Babe Ruth." Gibson fans disagreed. They said Ruth was "the white Josh Gibson."

Sadly, fans never got to see the two share the same field. Gibson played in an era in which Black players were not allowed in MLB. Gibson instead starred in the Negro Leagues. But anyone who did see Gibson play came away impressed. The powerful slugger was known for hitting home runs farther than anyone. That was how he got his start in pro baseball.

Gibson was sitting in the stands at a Homestead Grays game in Pittsburgh when their starting catcher got hurt. Gibson came down and filled in for the rest of the game. He quickly gained a reputation for hitting mammoth home runs. Gibson reportedly once hit a 580-foot (177-m) homer at Yankee Stadium. He was also a skilled catcher with a strong arm.

Nobody knows for sure just how good Gibson was. Negro League records were not always kept. But the Baseball Hall of Fame credits Gibson with nearly 800 career home runs. He also won multiple batting titles. Gibson's career was cut short when he died at the age of 35 in January 1947. Months later, Jackie Robinson debuted as the first Black MLB player of the twentieth century.

Joe DiMaggio poses for a photo during spring training in 1946. DiMaggio returned to MLB that season after missing three years while serving in the military.

JOE DIMAGGIO

From the moment he stepped onto an MLB field in 1936, Joe DiMaggio was more than just a baseball player. He was one of the biggest celebrities of his era. His marriage to actress Marilyn Monroe made him known to people who didn't even follow baseball. People who did follow baseball knew DiMaggio as one of the greatest all-around players ever.

The New York Yankees center fielder was given many nicknames during his Hall-of-Fame career. The two most popular were "Joltin' Joe" and "the Yankee Clipper."

DiMaggio won his first batting title in 1939. His .381 average was 21 points higher than second place. He won again the next year by hitting .352. DiMaggio could also hit for power. He slugged 29 or more home runs in each of his first six seasons.

DiMaggio is best known for what he did in the 1941 season. On May 14, DiMaggio failed to record a hit. That would not happen again until July 17. DiMaggio got at least one hit in 56 games in a row. That smashed the old AL record of 41 straight games.

No one in all of baseball has even reached 45 games since. DiMaggio's streak is considered to be one of the game's most unbreakable records. DiMaggio won his first of three Most Valuable Player (MVP) awards that season.

DiMaggio's career totals could have been even more impressive. However, he missed three seasons from 1943 to 1945 while serving in the military during World War II (1939–1945).

TED WILLIAMS

By the time Ted Williams joined the Boston Red Sox in 1939, hitting .400 in a season was becoming rare. Nobody had hit .400 in nine years. Williams would be the next. And for at least the next 80 years, he would be the last.

Williams spent all 19 seasons of his career with the Red Sox. The left fielder could always hit for average. He hit at least .300 in each season of his Hall-of-Fame career.

Williams spent most of the 1941 season near the .400 mark. Going into the last day of the year, a doubleheader, Williams was at .39955. If he sat out the last two games, his number would round up to .400. But Williams chose to play. He went 6-for-8 that day and ended up at .406.

That was only the start of Williams's career. He won five more batting titles. He hit for the Triple Crown twice. He won two AL MVPs and hit more than 500 home runs, including one in his final MLB at-bat.

Williams served as a Marine Corps pilot in World War II and the Korean War (1950–1953). As a result, he missed 1943 through 1945 and most of the 1952 and 1953 seasons. Williams retired at age 41 after another .300 season in 1960.

FAST FACT

The closest any player has come in the 80 years since Williams hit .400 was Tony Gwynn in 1994. Gwynn was hitting .394 in August before the rest of the season was canceled due to a player strike.

Even six decades after he retired, Ted Williams still held baseball's all-time best career on-base percentage of .482.

Stan Musial hit well everywhere. He had 1,815 career hits at home and 1,815 on the road.

STAN MUSIAL

For Stan Musial, the road to 24 All-Star Games started with a broomstick and a ball of tape. That was how a young Musial learned to hit. He practiced making the best contact he could over and over again.

Musial began his minor league career as a pitcher. In 1940 he spent some time filling in as an outfielder and hit .311. By the next year, he earned a call-up to the St. Louis Cardinals. He hit .426 in 12 games.

Musial missed the All-Star Game in that short season. He missed it the next year too, despite finishing twelfth in NL MVP voting. "Stan the Man" would make the All-Star team and win MVP during the 1943 season, though. And he would never miss another one. In his 22 years, the only other time he wasn't selected for an All-Star Game was in 1945. Musial was away from baseball serving in the Navy that season, but the game was also canceled.

Musial returned in 1946 to win his second NL MVP award. He would add a third in 1948. He also won seven NL batting titles. Even at the age of 41 in 1962, he hit .330 and finished third in the NL batting race.

When Musial retired, he held numerous NL records. He was the all-time leader in games played (3,026) and hits (3,630). He is still a beloved figure in St. Louis.

FAST FACT

Musial played in more All-Star Games than seasons in MLB. Baseball held two per season from 1959 to 1962. Musial played in all eight contests during that stretch.

After breaking baseball's color barrier in 1947, Robinson spent 10 years with the Dodgers, helping them win the World Series in 1955.

JACKIE ROBINSON

An MLB career was not an option for Jackie Robinson coming out of University of California, Los Angeles (UCLA), in the early 1940s. Segregation was common throughout the United States, and the league did not allow Black players. Robinson didn't seem like a future baseball star anyway. He played only one season with the Bruins and hit .097.

After leaving the Army, he decided to give baseball another try. He joined the Kansas City Monarchs of the Negro Leagues in 1945. This time he excelled. Brooklyn Dodgers general manager Branch Rickey took notice. Rickey believed Black players could thrive in MLB. But the first one would have to be both good and strong-willed in order to withstand the abuse that would follow. Rickey believed he had the right man in Robinson. He offered Robinson a contract with the Dodgers' top farm team in Montreal.

Robinson displayed a special blend of hitting ability and speed. He led the International League in average and was second in stolen bases in 1946. In 1947 Robinson got the call that he was going to the Dodgers.

Robinson made his MLB debut on April 15, 1947. He was the league's first Black player in over 60 years. Hostile crowds greeted him at games. Even some Dodgers players said they wouldn't play with a Black teammate. But Robinson's mental toughness and smooth skill won fans during his 10-year career. He was a six-time All-Star and won the 1949 batting title. He also led the NL in stolen bases twice.

Jackie Robinson Day is observed throughout MLB every April 15. Every on-field player wears Robinson's No. 42, which has also been retired by every team.

WILLIE MAYS

Willie Mays began in the Negro Leagues in the late 1940s. He made his MLB debut in 1951 but was drafted into the military in 1952. Finally, in 1954, Mays came back for good. He proved to be worth the wait. Behind his MVP season, the New York Giants made it all the way to the World Series.

In Game 1, Mays made one of the most famous catches in baseball history. He sprinted to the outfield wall and caught the ball over his shoulder to keep the game tied. Mays and the Giants went on to win the series. And a superstar was born.

Throughout baseball history, few could compare to Mays's all-around ability. He played a dazzling style of baseball. The centerfielder led the NL in stolen bases four times and triples three times. He hit at least 40 home runs in six different seasons, topping out at 52 in 1965. The player known as "the Say Hey Kid" was also breathtaking in center field. Mays's flashy glove work and strong arm won him 12 Gold Glove Awards. On top of his unmatched skills, his joyful personality and love of playing brought fans to the ballpark.

In 1958 the Giants moved to San Francisco. Mays went along, ultimately playing 21 seasons with the franchise. He finished his career back in New York with the Mets in 1972 and 1973. There he collected the final 14 of his 660 career home runs. That ranked third in league history when he retired.

Mays was elected to the Hall of Fame in 1979. When the Giants opened their current ballpark in 2000, the address was made 24 Willie Mays Plaza.

Willie Mays leaps to make a catch during spring training in 1958. An exceptional fielder, Mays won 12 Gold Glove Awards in his career.

Mantle's 536 home runs are the most ever by a switch hitter.

MICKEY MANTLE

Mickey Mantle had some big shoes to fill. He stepped into center field for the New York Yankees in 1952. That was a position previously held by Joe DiMaggio.

No one would ever forget "Joltin' Joe." But Mantle made a legacy of his own. He was one of baseball's greatest power hitters. He hit a lot of home runs. But he also hit them a long way.

Mantle hit one of the longest home runs in baseball history on April 17, 1953. At Griffith Stadium against the Washington Senators, Mantle hit the ball clear out of the ballpark. It finally landed 565 feet (172 m) from home plate. The term "tape-measure home run" was born that day.

Mantle led the AL in homers four times. In 1956 he won the AL Triple Crown with a .353 average, 52 home runs, and 130 RBIs. Mantle won his first AL MVP Award that year. He won it again in 1957 and 1962. "The Mick" struck fear into opposing pitchers. As his reputation grew, opposing pitchers did their best to avoid his big bat. Mantle lead the league in walks five times.

Injuries were the only thing that could slow Mantle down. The slugger dealt with many of them in his 18-year career. Knee problems especially took their toll. He played much of his career on one healthy leg.

Despite being one of baseball's biggest superstars, Mantle was known for his humble personality. He was helpful to rookies and respected by his teammates. Mantle was inducted into the Hall of Fame in 1974.

Hank Aaron holds up the ball he hit for his then record-setting 715th home run.

HENRY "HANK" AARON

Few records in sports matter more to baseball fans than the all-time home run record. And for decades, that record belonged to Babe Ruth. The Babe was baseball royalty. He was also white. When a Black player like Hank Aaron challenged the record in the 1970s, some people didn't like it.

Aaron had been on track to pass Ruth for years. He started in the Negro Leagues and was already a great player when he debuted for the Milwaukee Braves in 1954. Three years later, he was named the NL MVP. For the most part, though, Aaron was a quiet, steady performer. He never hit more than 47 home runs in a season. But he hit 30 or more 15 times. He also made a record-setting 25 All-Star teams.

By the time the Braves moved to Atlanta in 1966, Aaron was creeping up on Ruth's record. He finished the 1973 season one home run shy of tying Ruth. People targeted Aaron with racist abuse that offseason, including hate mail and death threats.

But plenty of fans were excited about the home run chase. Big crowds came out to catch a glimpse of history. Aaron tied Ruth at 714 on opening day in 1974. Four days later, on April 8, a packed home crowd of 53,775 came out to see whether Aaron could pass the Babe. In the fourth inning, Aaron launched a drive off the Los Angeles Dodgers' Al Downing deep into the Georgia night.

Aaron played two more seasons and finished with 755 career home runs. No one would challenge that mark for more than 30 years.

ROBERTO CLEMENTE

Latino players are now some of MLB's greatest stars. But they were rare when Roberto Clemente joined the Pittsburgh Pirates in 1955. Clemente was born in the United States on the island territory of Puerto Rico. He spoke little English when his career began, but his graceful all-around play did much of the talking for him. It also inspired many future Latino players to dream of playing in the big leagues.

Clemente batted .317 over his 18-year career with the Pittsburgh Pirates. He won the NL batting title four times. The right fielder hit 240 home runs and added 166 triples. Clemente was also known for his stylish fielding and cannon right arm. Those skills helped him earn 12 Gold Glove Awards in his career.

Clemente shone brightest in the World Series, which he won twice with the Pirates. His play in the 1971 series against the Baltimore Orioles ranks as one of the best postseason performances of all time. Clemente hit .414 with two doubles, a triple, and two home runs. His second homer broke a scoreless tie in Game 7. Clemente recorded at least one hit in all 14 World Series games he played.

Clemente got his 3,000th hit on September 30, 1972. Sadly, it would be his last. That winter he was traveling to Nicaragua to aid victims of an earthquake when his plane crashed in the Atlantic Ocean. Upon his death, the voting committee waived the traditional waiting period and inducted Clemente immediately into the Hall of Fame.

Roberto Clemente poses for a photo during the 1967 season. Clemente hit .357 that year, the best average of his 18-year career.

Roger Clemens pitched in the World Series for the Boston Red Sox, New York Yankees, and Houston Astros.

ROGER CLEMENS

Every year the best pitcher in each league receives the Cy Young Award. It is named after the pitching great from baseball's early years. Roger Clemens has won that award seven times, the most of any pitcher. The records set by Young himself are unlikely ever to be matched. But few players have come as close as Clemens. Clemens is the only pitcher in history to record 350 or more wins and at least 4,500 strikeouts.

The man nicknamed "the Rocket" did not need a lot of different pitches to get hitters out. Clemens relied mostly on a scorching fastball. He was an intimidating presence on the mound, and he made hitters uncomfortable.

Clemens had a long career. He remained a dominant pitcher even into his 40s. Clemens struck out a record 20 batters in a game in 1986. He did it again 10 years later. Only three other pitchers have ever recorded 20 strikeouts in a nine-inning game. At the age of 42 in 2004, Clemens became the oldest pitcher to win a Cy Young Award.

Numbers like Clemens's would normally mean an automatic spot in the Hall of Fame. But Clemens was accused of using performance-enhancing drugs (PEDs) during his career. Clemens has denied ever using the drugs. But the accusations have kept him out of the Hall.

FAST FACT

Clemens and Young are tied for most wins in Boston Red Sox history. Each won 192 games in Boston, roughly 90 years apart.

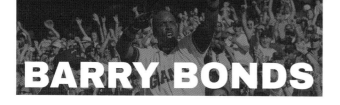

BARRY BONDS

Barry Bonds was born into baseball royalty. His father, Bobby, was a big leaguer. His godfather, Willie Mays, was maybe the greatest all-around player in history. The younger Bonds would soon go on to rival them.

Bonds spent less than a year in the minor leagues. With a rare blend of speed and power, he quickly made an impact in the majors. Bonds debuted with the Pittsburgh Pirates in 1986. By 1990 he was the NL MVP. He won a second MVP two years later.

In 1993 Bonds signed as a free agent with the San Francisco Giants, the same team where Mays had spent most of his career. Bonds won another MVP that season. In 1996 Bonds became the first NL player ever to have 40 or more home runs and 40 or more stolen bases in the same season. In all, Bonds had five seasons of at least 30 homers and 30 steals. That was a feat matched only by his father, Bobby.

As Bonds aged, his stolen bases declined. But his lightning-quick bat remained the same. Bonds transformed into one of the best sluggers in baseball history. He broke the single-season home run record in 2001 with 73. He won the MVP that season and the next three seasons in a row.

In 2007 Bonds broke the all-time home run record. He finished his career with 762. However, the achievement was not widely celebrated. He had been accused of using PEDs later in his career. Bonds denied using PEDs and never failed a test.

FAST FACT

The single-season home run record was set twice in four years. Before Bonds claimed the record in 2001, St. Louis's Mark McGwire and Chicago's Sammy Sosa both chased it in 1998. At that time, McGwire set the new mark with 70, and Sosa had 66.

Barry Bonds celebrates with San Francisco Giants fans after leading the team to the 1997 National League West title.

MARIANO RIVERA

Mariano Rivera was not the first closer in baseball. But he made an art form out of locking down wins in the ninth inning. No pitcher in MLB history recorded as many saves.

Rivera did not start out as a reliever. When he debuted with the Yankees in 1995, he started 10 games. But with Rivera's history of elbow problems, the Yankees thought a move to relief pitcher might be a better option. Rivera made his playoff debut that year, pitching 3 1/3 innings in his first game and earning the win.

That was the first of many outstanding playoff performances as a reliever. Rivera allowed just a single run in the 1996 playoffs, as the Yankees won the World Series. By 1997 Rivera had become the full-time closer. He earned 647 of his record 652 saves over the next 17 years.

Rivera had good speed on his fastball. But speed was not his key to success. He threw a cut fastball that had more movement. The pitch baffled hitters and kept them off balance.

FAST FACT

Mariano Rivera was the last MLB player to wear Jackie Robinson's No. 42 every day. He was wearing it when the number was retired in 1997 and was allowed to continue for the rest of his career.

Rivera was outstanding in the regular season. But he was even better in the playoffs. He had 42 career postseason saves and a 0.70 earned-run average. Both marks are MLB records.

In 2019 Rivera became eligible for the Hall of Fame. Every single voter cast a ballot for him. That made him the first unanimous selection in the Hall's history.

Hitters knew Mariano Rivera's cut fastball was coming. But they still struggled to hit it.

Albert Pujols smacks one of his three home runs against the Chicago Cubs during a game on July 20, 2004.

ALBERT PUJOLS

Young third baseman Albert Pujols was impressive in spring training in 2001. But it wasn't certain he would make the St. Louis Cardinals roster. His teammates made it clear they wanted him around. One even told manager Tony La Russa it would be the biggest mistake of his career to cut Pujols.

Days later La Russa put Pujols's name in the Opening Day lineup. Pujols's name would be on more than 2,800 more lineup cards over the course of his career. And he kept slugging his way toward the Hall of Fame.

Pujols played like a combination of Hank Aaron and Willie Mays. He possessed a rare blend of contact hitting and power. As a Cardinal, he won three NL MVPs in 10 years. In that stretch, he hit at least .300 with 30 or more home runs and 100 or more RBIs every year.

Pujols moved on to the Los Angeles Angels in his early 30s. He no longer hit for average as he once did. But he continued to show power and was a consistent presence in the lineup. As he entered his 40s, he started to rank among some all-time greats.

Pujols became the thirty-second member of the 3,000-hit club in 2018. In 2020 Pujols moved into the top five on the all-time home runs list. He hit his 661st homer to pass Mays. Twenty years after his manager took a risk on Pujols as a rookie, the slugger cemented his place as one of the greats.

MIKE TROUT

Mike Trout was only 19 when he debuted for the Los Angeles Angels in 2011. It wasn't the start he hoped for. That season the outfielder hit just .220 in 40 games. The Angels decided to start him in the minor leagues the next year. It didn't take Trout long to earn another shot. The Angels called him up just one month into the 2012 season. From that moment, he showed he was one of MLB's best players.

Trout won AL Rookie of the Year in 2012 and was MVP runner-up. He hit for both average and power. He hit 30 home runs, and he also led the major leagues with 49 stolen bases. He was instantly one of the best center fielders in the game. His leaping grab to steal a home run from Baltimore Orioles shortstop J. J. Hardy on June 27 that year was one of his early memorable moments.

It was only a matter of time before Trout started piling up even more awards. He won his first MVP in 2014 at age 22. He hit 36 home runs and led the AL in both runs scored and RBIs.

Trout has drawn comparisons to several greats. His speed and power bring to mind Mickey Mantle. His hitting ability has reminded fans of Ted Williams. He led the AL in on-base percentage each year from 2016 to 2019. During that stretch, he added two more MVP awards. Trout finished no lower than fifth in AL MVP voting in each of his first nine full MLB seasons.

Trout hit his 300th career home run at 29 years old on September 5, 2020. He was the eleventh-youngest player to reach that mark, behind only greats like Albert Pujols, Mickey Mantle, and Hank Aaron.

Mike Trout started drawing comparisons to other all-time greats after just a few years in MLB.

HONORABLE MENTIONS

ROGERS HORNSBY

Hornsby was a tough second baseman who holds the modern-era single-season batting average record of .424, set in 1924.

MEL OTT

One of the NL's best sluggers of the 1930s and '40s, Ott became the first NL player to hit 500 home runs.

FRANK ROBINSON

The 1966 Triple Crown winner, Robinson won the MVP in both leagues and finished with 586 career home runs.

TOM SEAVER

Seaver was the hero of the 1969 New York Mets' World Series victory. He won 311 games and three Cy Young Awards over 20 seasons.

JOHNNY BENCH

Bench was one of the greatest catchers of all time both offensively and defensively. Before retiring in 1983, he hit 389 career homers and won 10 Gold Gloves.

RICKEY HENDERSON

Henderson's 1,406 stolen bases are nearly 500 more than any other player. He also scored an MLB-record 2,295 runs in his 25-year career that ended in 2003.

CAL RIPKEN JR.

Known as the "Iron Man" shortstop, Ripken broke Lou Gehrig's consecutive games streak in 1995.

RANDY JOHNSON

Johnson is second all-time in career strikeouts. Before retiring in 2009, he established himself as one of only six lefties to win 300 career games.

GLOSSARY

ace
A team's best starting pitcher.

batting average
A player's number of hits divided by the number of at-bats.

closer
A pitcher who comes in at the end of the game to secure a win for his team.

competitive
Desiring to win, or having as fair of a chance to win as one's opponents.

curveball
A pitch that slightly changes direction during its flight toward the plate.

earned-run average
A statistic that measures the average number of earned runs that a pitcher gives up per nine innings.

Gold Glove Award
An award that recognizes the top fielder in the league at each position.

postseason
The playoffs, including the wild-card round, divisional playoffs, league championship series, and World Series.

relief
An appearance by a pitcher who does not start the game.

rookie
A professional athlete in his or her first year of competition.

sportsmanship
Fair and generous behavior or treatment of others in a sports contest.

stolen base
Running from one base to another during a pitch, not during a hit.

MORE INFORMATION

BOOKS

Gitlin, Marty. *Baseball Underdog Stories*. Minneapolis, MN: Abdo
Publishing, 2019.

Gitlin, Marty. *Great Baseball Debates*. Minneapolis, MN: Abdo Publishing, 2019.

Harris, Duchess. *Jackie Robinson Breaks Barriers*. Minneapolis, MN: Abdo
Publishing, 2019.

ONLINE RESOURCES

To learn more about the GOATs of baseball, please visit
abdobooklinks.com or scan this QR code. These links are
routinely monitored and updated to provide the most current
information available.

INDEX

ABOUT THE AUTHOR

Anthony K. Hewson is a freelance writer originally from San Diego. He and his wife now live in the San Francisco Bay Area with their two dogs.